The 91st Psalm

Illustrated by Stefanie Palmer

WestBow Press books may be ordered through booksellers or by contacting:

WestBow Press
A Division of Thomas Nelson & Zondervan
1663 Liberty Drive
Bloomington, IN 47403
www.westbowpress.com
1 (844) 714-3454

The Illustrator's Insights at the back of the book are written by Stefanie Palmer.

All illustrations are original watercolour and gouache paintings on paper by Stefanie Palmer.

ISBN: 978-1-5127-5999-0 (sc)
ISBN: 978-1-5127-5998-3 (e)

Library of Congress Control Number: 2016916609

Print information available on the last page.

WestBow Press rev. date: 10/22/2020

For all those seeking comfort.

He that dwelleth in the secret place
of the most High shall abide under the
shadow of the Almighty.

I will say of the Lord,
He is my refuge and my fortress:
my God; in him will I trust.

**Surely he shall deliver thee
from the snare of the fowler,
and from the noisome pestilence.**

He shall cover thee with his feathers,
and under his wings shalt thou trust:
his truth shall be thy shield and buckler.

Thou shalt not be afraid for the terror by night;
nor for the arrow that flieth by day;
Nor for the pestilence that walketh in darkness;
nor for the destruction that wasteth at noonday.

A thousand shall fall at thy side,
and ten thousand at thy right hand;
but it shall not come nigh thee.

Only with thine eyes shalt thou behold
and see the reward of the wicked.

Because thou hast made the Lord,
which is my refuge,
even the most High,
thy habitation;

There shall no evil befall thee, neither shall any plague come nigh thy dwelling.

For he shall give his angels charge over thee,
to keep thee in all thy ways.
They shall bear thee up in their hands,
lest thou dash thy foot against a stone.

**Thou shalt tread upon the lion and adder:
the young lion and the dragon
shalt thou trample under feet.**

Because he hath set his love upon me,
therefore will I deliver him:
I will set him on high,
because he hath known my name.

He shall call upon me,
and I will answer him:
I will be with him in trouble;
I will deliver him, and honour him.

With long life will I satisfy him,
and shew him my salvation.

Illustrator's Insights

Kangaroos are native to Australia. The babies are called joeys and are only about 2cm / 0.8in long when they are born. They hide in their mother's pouch drinking milk and growing until they are about 9 months old.

People have used snares to trap birds for thousands of years, but this chicken is not going to be fooled.

Baby swans are called cygnets and are protected by both of their parents.

Fawn is both the name of a young deer and their yellowish-brown colour.

Koalas and kangaroos are marsupials and their babies share the name of joey. Piggybacks from mum are very popular with young koalas, and if you look closely, you will find a kookaburra sitting in the gumtree.

Here one greedy squirrel is chittering at another but is about to learn a lesson in sharing acorns.

These mountain goats are like those I have seen in the Colorado Rocky Mountains. The young are called kids and are excellent mountaineers.

This wombat has stayed safe in her burrow during a bushfire. By her feet, there is a banksia seedpod that needed the fire to open it to release its seeds.

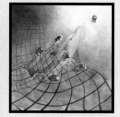

Discarded or lost fishing nets are called ghost nets and sea life get tangled in them. This dolphin is being rescued by some angelfish.

Having "dominion" (Gen 1:26) is to not be afraid but rather be loving and at peace with all creatures. "The wolf also shall dwell with the lamb, and the leopard shall lie down with the kid; and the calf and the young lion and the fatling together; and a little child shall lead them" (Isaiah 11:6).

Dunnarts are Australian mouse-sized marsupials that express God's qualities of listening and watching with their big ears and eyes.

Macaws are beautiful birds that can live more than 100 years. They are native to Central and South America and Mexico.

The End

The Illustrator

Stefanie "Sten" Palmer is an Australian who earned her Bachelor of Arts Degree, with a major in Studio Art and minors in Education and Religion, from Principia College, USA. While there, Glenn Felch instructed her in the art of watercolour illustration for which she is eternally grateful.

Sten loves encouraging others to feel divinely inspired by nature and has led many children and adults on peak trips in the Colorado Rocky Mountains and on sea kayaking expeditions along the Ningaloo Reef in Western Australia. Solo time in nature is one of her favourite activities.

Printed in the United States
By Bookmasters